Lines in
Long Array

—————

Lines in Long Array

A Civil War Commemoration

POEMS AND PHOTOGRAPHS
Past and Present

Edited by David C. Ward and Frank H. Goodyear III

National Portrait Gallery
Washington, D.C.

Distributed by Smithsonian Books. This book may be purchased for educational, business, or sales promotional use. For information please write: Smithsonian Books, Special Markets, P.O. Box 37012, MRC 513, Washington, DC 20013.

Printed in Spain, not at government expense

Library of Congress Control Number: 2013936583
ISBN: 978-1-58834-397-0

Interior details:
p. 2: *Breaking Camp, Brandy Station, Virginia* (detail) by Alexander Gardner, 1864. Photographic History Collection, National Museum of American History, Smithsonian Institution. Reproduced in full on p. 119.
p. 10: *Abraham Lincoln* ("cracked-plate" image) (detail) by Alexander Gardner, 1865. National Portrait Gallery, Smithsonian Institution. Reproduced in full on back flap.
p. 14: *A Burial Party, Cold Harbor, Virginia* (detail) by Alexander Gardner, 1865. Photographic History Collection, National Museum of American History, Smithsonian Institution. Reproduced in full on p. 125.
p. 18: *Untitled* (#20 Chancellorsville) (detail) from *Last Measure* by Sally Mann, 2002. Collection of the artist. Reproduced in full on p. 97.
p. 100: *Ruins of Arsenal, Richmond, Virginia* (detail) by Alexander Gardner, 1865. Photographic History Collection, National Museum of American History, Smithsonian Institution. Reproduced in full on p. 123.

Editorial and production management: Dru Dowdy, Head of Publications, National Portrait Gallery
Design: Studio A, Alexandria, Virginia
Printing: Syl Creaciones Gráficas Barcelona, Spain

This project was supported with funds from the Smithsonian Institution's Consortium for Understanding the American Experience.

Contents

Preface

Lines in Long Array was conceived as part of the Smithsonian Institution's coverage of the 150th anniversary of the Civil War. In addition to the institution's historical programming on the war, we thought it would be interesting and appropriate to commission a group of contemporary poets to offer their artistic reflections on the war, history, and memory. In one sense, we wanted this volume to be a memorial—a commemoration—but we also wanted it to be a living document that created cultural connections between our time and the generation of the war itself. Instead of a historical consideration of the war, we wanted an artistic one.

We were inspired in part by a historic precedent. In the North during the war, at least two large works were published that collected writings from the leading authors of the day and from earlier in the Republic's history. *Autograph Leaves of Our Country's Authors* (1864) is a collection of poems and essays, and *A Tribute to the Fair: Comprising a Collection of Vers de Société* (1864) contains poems published to support the United States Sanitary Commission. These volumes aimed both to help raise money for those who were suffering during the war and to solicit writing that would say something important about the times. We think that a similar work today says something interesting about our era, as well as about our memory of the Civil War.

We have organized this volume around poetry and photography because during the war, American society—North and South—used those two mediums to attempt to organize and understand their thoughts about contemporary events. The poetry of the time, from Walt Whitman to popular songs, is woven into the fabric of American culture. And it was through the immediacy of the new discipline of photography that the reality of war was transmitted from the battleground to the home front by such artists as Alexander Gardner and Mathew Brady.

Our thoughts were not to create a comprehensive survey or anthology. Rather, we wanted to create an artistic reengagement with the past by asking current artists to reconsider the war from today's vantage point. We asked twelve eminent poets to write about anything about the war that excited their imagination, setting no restrictions on length, topic, or form. For the visual complement to the verbal, we asked photographer Sally Mann to let us publish her evocative representations of Civil War battlescapes from the series *Last Measure*.

Against these modern works of art, we counterpoised examples in poetry and photography from the time. We chose twelve poems that stand on their own but also give a sense of the state of American verse in the mid- to late nineteenth century. Our selection includes harbingers of modernism alongside fine examples of Victorian sentimentality. For the historic photographs, we have for the most part utilized Alexander Gardner's *Photographic Sketch Book of the War*, choosing images that are singular in their visual impact and work well in relation to the poems. In two short essays we have provided some amplification of our thoughts as historians and curators on the war and poetry and photography. Our intention, again, was not to be comprehensive but imaginative: we want this volume to expand our ideas about how we continue to think about—and rethink—the Civil War. Throughout, our guide has been William Faulkner's artistic credo, "The past isn't dead; it isn't even past."

"The Real War ...": Poetry and the Civil War

David C. Ward

Walt Whitman wrote two memorial poems for Abraham Lincoln. One, "O Captain, My Captain," is a fine piece of Victorian sentimentality, much anthologized and much recited on patriotic occasions:

> This dust was once the Man,
> Gentle, plain, just and resolute—under whose cautious hand,
> Against the foulest crime in history known in any land or age,
> Was saved the Union of These States.

Whitman would recite the poem at the conclusion of his public lecture "The Death of Lincoln," and he grew weary of it. If "O Captain, My Captain" was rooted in the poetic vocabulary of mid-nineteenth-century conventionality, Whitman's second Lincoln poem, "When Lilacs Last in the Dooryard Bloom'd," vaulted American poetry toward the future, creating a decisive break, both linguistically and in its cast of mind, with the time in which he wrote. It is a hallucinatory work that is as close as an American poet has ever gotten to Dante's journey into the Underworld:

> Passing the visions, passing the night;
> Passing, unloosing the hold of my comrades' hands;
> Passing the song of the hermit bird, and the tallying song of my soul
> Victorious song, death's outlet song, yet varying, ever-altering song,
> As low and wailing yet clear the notes, rising and falling, flooding the night ...

Although Whitman himself wrote many fine poems about the Civil War, the two extremes represented by his Lincoln poems illustrate how the war itself disappears from American verse: it is either swaddled in pieties that indicate a kind of emotional incomprehension, or it becomes the jumping-off point for an incipient modernism, one that leaves the war and the past behind. As Whitman himself put it, "The real war will not get in the books." Or as T. S. Eliot put it rather more grandiloquently, "Between the idea / And the reality / Falls the Shadow."

The Civil War is the great shadow in American literature. It exists historically, of course, as fact—even when those facts are hotly contested—and it is a staple of popular forms of genre fiction, from romance novels to cowboy stories, that thrive on melodrama. But its traces in the national literature are slight: Faulkner (of course), Stephen Crane, poems by Emily Dickinson or Allen Tate or Robert Lowell. The war has simply not received the direct attention that one would have expected it to receive from America's writers. Yet it exerts its influence over our literature indirectly and seems to shadow everything that comes after it, precisely because it is excluded as a subject.

Edmund Wilson wrote a very influential chapter in *Patriotic Gore* about how the war changed American language by making it more concise, lapidary, and crisp. The language of military orders then influenced literary diction. But more broadly, the conciseness of this language indicated an emotional repression caused by the trauma of the war. This "real" war could not be in the books because it was too overwhelming to be comprehended. Where would someone even begin? So it was excised and pushed aside to invisibly influence the direction of American culture and society, like the gravitational pull of some huge, unseen planet. The war was simply too tragic, and Americans don't do tragedy. The structure of *Huckleberry Finn* (1884) is indicative. The novel is unbalanced: chapters of lyrical landscape writing as Huck and Jim float down the river alternate with comic scenes of the American grotesque once they come ashore. Twain can only write about American history by burlesquing it. Huck and Jim escape history on the river; Twain escapes it through comedy—and the ending, which gestures satirically at the politics of Reconstruction, is a cheat.

The very opposite occurs in the case of the South and southern writing, which helps support this argument. Having experienced defeat and the extinction of their way of life, southerners had to confront the consequence of the tragedy and their fall; hence Faulkner's great paean in *Intruder in the Dust* (1948) to the "Lost Cause":

There is the instant when it's still not yet two o'clock on that July afternoon in 1863, the brigades are in position behind the rail fence, the guns are laid and ready in the woods and the furled flags are already loosened to break out and Pickett himself with his long oiled ringlets and his hat in one hand probably and his sword in the other looking up the hill waiting for Longstreet to give the word and it's all in the balance, it hasn't happened yet, it hasn't even begun yet, it not only hasn't begun yet but there is still time for it not to begin against that position and those circumstances.

It hadn't "happened yet," but it did. From that moment on—there is a monument at Gettysburg to the "High Tide of the Confederacy"—the South was forced to keep looking backwards, addressing the wound and nursing its grievances. The North could afford to turn away, bury the past, acknowledge that something had happened without considering exactly what it was. This evasion redoubled in force once the goal of equality for African Americans was abandoned with the end of Reconstruction.

It is the Civil War, not World War I as is commonly argued, that began the transition to a modernist America, a modernism that Whitman announces in "When Lilacs Last." It leaves its imprint in Stephen Crane and becomes a full-fledged literary movement in writers like Ezra Pound and Henry James, a movement that will determine the course of American writing for a century. It is a tradition of great power and virtuosity; it is a literature in which America can be said to have come of artistic age. But it is a tradition built on a great omission: the Civil War that brought it into being.

Shattered Ground: Photography and the Civil War

Frank H. Goodyear III

Photographers who go to war are no mere illustrators. By the nature of their practice they participate as frontline soldiers, except that their primary tool is a camera rather than a gun. They head out to bear witness to often-cataclysmic events and invariably return affected by their experience. Their photographs are shaped by the range of emotion that war produces: hope and anger, triumph and sadness, anxiety and boredom.

With the advent of photography on the eve of the American Civil War, war received a wholly new face. Photographs provided an original and unsettling perspective on an age-old subject. After centuries of imagery that heroicized war, photography replaced mythic notions with upsetting new truths: namely, that combat was no teapot drama but rather a long, agonizing struggle. Present on the frontlines, these image-makers introduced new narratives about the experience of being a soldier and, alongside other changes wrought by the Industrial Revolution, contributed to a sea-change in society's understanding about war.

Alexander Gardner's *Photographic Sketch Book of the War*, published in 1866, a year following the South's surrender, attempted to relate a new type of history. Centered on photographs created by Gardner and a team of colleagues, this two-volume work aspired to narrate the history of the conflict through one hundred images completed over the previous four years. Although Gardner, an immigrant from Paisley, Scotland, gave titles to each picture and introduced captions—perhaps fearing that readers might not fully understand the images without some type of written description—it was the photographs that were the focus of this history. Gardner and others had circulated views of the battlefield during the conflict itself, but Gardner's *Photographic Sketch Book of the War* was something altogether new: a history of the full conflict rendered through this new visual technology. These images and their use as records in a larger documentary narrative broke new ground in terms of photography's creative potential. Replete with ruin and death, they also marked a stark transformation from earlier literary and visual accounts of war and its participants.

Although Gardner's work ushered in a new era, his photographs should be regarded as fragments—incomplete remnants of battles waged. They tell only part of the story. Gardner and his colleagues made visible the wide swath of destruction left in the Union army's wake. Yet they focused less on other elements of the war, including the fate of the wounded, the displaced, and others on the margins of the conflict. Additionally, he never photographed alongside the Confederate army. How could he, of course, given who he was? No less true then as today, frontline photographers record what is available and what seems compelling at a specific time. Gardner's views create rich, often disturbing narratives about selective moments during this extraordinary war. Seen together, they highlight the experience of being present at these sites.

Almost a century and a half later, photographer Sally Mann revisited some of the places where those bitterly fought battles played out. Many have trod these lands, and although the names of most casualties have long since been lost, the memory of the human presence at these sites continues. Mann lives in Lexington, Virginia, the heart of one of the most contested regions during the war. Her landscapes, though unpeopled, evoke those who were once there. They bring forward the scarring that nature can hide and mankind can alter, but that neither can ever completely erase. Employing the wet-plate collodion photographic process—the same practiced by Gardner—she creates images that grapple with the layers of history inscribed on these fields and the emotional resonance that adheres there. While Gardner and his contemporaries would have deemed the streaks, scars, and spots that appear in her photographs as imperfections, to Mann they animate the landscape, suggesting tracings of otherworldly forces.

Much exists that the eye cannot see, and Mann's photographs ponder what lies beyond traditional human sight. These landscapes—part of a series titled *Last Measure*—reveal that the medium can see below the surface of things and strike through the pasteboard masks to capture echoes from the past and unseen markings from the present. At Gettysburg in 1863, President Lincoln honored the dead who had given "the last full measure of devotion" to the Union cause. Working at places such as Antietam, Fredericksburg, and Appomattox, Mann considers anew what happened at such sites 150 years ago and how memories of that time continue to cling to our imagination. War never disappears from the land and the people. Although the traces can sometimes seem faint, her photographs capture the cacophony of voices that fill these sites.

During the Civil War, more than a million people died or were wounded. In photographs from that period and today, the trauma of that conflict continues. Gardner and Mann remind us that these events shaped that generation and every other since then.

POEMS, 2012–13

Tulsa

John Koethe

> Always treat humanity, whether in
> yourself or in another person, as an end
> in itself, and never simply as a means.
>   Kant

It wasn't just the slaughter—though proportionally it
Exceeded all our other wars combined—but what prefigured it
And what it brought about. There was the cotton gin
That gave the South a one-commodity economy
It needed slaves to run. And slavery required power,
Political power, to perpetuate itself, and power depended on
New slave states to sustain it, so that when its grandiose fantasy
Of Manifest Destiny—a Caribbean empire absorbing Mexico and Cuba—
Collapsed by 1861, there wasn't anything left to do but to secede.
It's sickening to read the rationales, because they cut so close. Mississippi:
"Our position is thoroughly identified with the institution of slavery—
The greatest material interest of the world. Its labor supplies the product
Which constitutes by far the largest and most important portions
Of commerce of the earth. These products are peculiar to the climate
Verging on the tropical regions, and by an imperious law of nature,
None but the black race can bear exposure to the tropical sun.
These products have become necessities to the world,
And a blow at slavery is a blow at commerce and civilization."
Georgia: "Because by their declared principles and policy
They have outlawed $3,000,000,000 of our property." Texas:
"That in this free government all white men are and of right
Ought to be entitled to equal civil and political rights;
That the servitude of the African race, as existing in these states,
Is mutually beneficial to both bond and free, and is abundantly authorized
And justified by the experience of mankind, and the revealed
Will of the Almighty Creator, as recognized by all Christian nations."

After a desultory start the carnage began in earnest, with standing charges—
The strategy Napoleon had used—into the teeth of modern ordnance
Scattering brains and blood and shattered bones across the open fields,
Until supplanted by the trenches that looked out upon the graves of WWI.
Sometimes the history of a war obscures the meaning of the war:
Behind the strategies and battles—Antietam and Gettysburg of course,
But also those whose names have vanished into books or onto Wikipedia,
Like Pebbles' Farm or Phillippi or Darbytown or Hoover's Gap—
The unconcluded narrative continued to unfold, conceived
In an original sin no ordinary victory or surrender could erase.
So when that victory finally came and the South gave up,
It was outwardly abolished, and the economic order it sustained
Went with the wind; but the souls of those who wrote those rationales
Remained unvanquished. As the bickering began, fatigue set in
And Reconstruction foundered. The Redeemers persevered,
The White League and the Red Shirts' organized campaigns of terror
Culminated in the Mississippi Plan of 1875, when the besieged
Republican electorate was shot or forced to flee, and Grant,
Fretting about Ohio, declined to intervene. The plan became a model
For the other states—South Carolina signed on too—until rendered obsolete
By the Compromise of 1877—the "Corrupt Bargain"—when in return
For the Presidency, Rutherford B. Hayes agreed to pull all Federal troops
From the South, which became, in effect, a separate nation after all.

That's the history part. I guess it's cynical and open to dispute:
There's the legend of the Lost Cause, that romanticized the way of life
The war destroyed, and whiggish history, in which whites somehow forgot
"That blacks were creating thriving middle classes in many states of the South."
In 1999 I flew to Tulsa for a literary festival. There was the small city's
Usual downtown whose best days were behind it, and Oral Roberts University's
Enormous praying hands that pointed straight at heaven. The people
Who'd invited me showed me the sights (including those gigantic hands),
And during lunch one day described the riots that occurred in 1921.
There was a vibrant black community in a part of town called Greenwood
(One of those thriving middle classes I suppose), so prosperous with its
Banks and businesses and homes that it was called "the Negro Wall Street."
On Memorial Day there was an incident in an elevator in a downtown building
That involved a young white woman and a young black man, who was jailed
On suspicion of assault. A white crowd gathered, incited by an editorial
In the *Tulsa Tribune* egging on a lynching. Skirmishes ensued,
And then at last a huge white mob stormed into Greenwood, shooting

Indiscriminately, burning stores and businesses and houses, while biplanes
From an airfield near town, left over from WWI, dropped firebombs
And fired at people on the ground, until the Negro Wall Street lay in ruins.
No one really knows many died—hundreds probably, and thousands wounded.
There's a modest monument today where Greenwood used to be,
But for over half a century the Tulsa Race Riot simply disappeared from history:
The copies of the *Tribune* with the editorial are missing from its archives
And the archives in the capitol; the riot itself went missing from the school
And history books, not just in Oklahoma and the South, but everywhere;
And there were never reparations. What flabbergasted me, beyond the riot itself,
Bad as it was, was the fact of its effacement, and the underlying explanation.
Dick Rowland—that was the young man's name—was just a stand-in
For the real cause: the black community's continually accumulating wealth,
That made its partial ownership of the oil companies that composed
The city's soul almost inevitable, but which was unacceptable. And so the
Pent up anger was unleashed, and the worst episode of racial
Violence in the country's history vanished completely from its past.

In metaphysics and philosophy of language there's a view that holds
That if you want to know what something is, ignore what people say about it—
Look instead at where it came from. So much of what has plagued our
Politics for centuries now—the distrust of reason and the common good, of the ideal
Of justice; the obsession with the perfidy of government, a base conception of the social order—
Descended from the original sin of slavery and the desperate struggle to maintain it,
Before taking on a life of its own. "There goes the South for a generation,"
Johnson said in 1964, though he was overly optimistic. The rhetoric
Of freedom floats upon the surface of a dark, unspoken dream of restoration,
Of a way of life that never actually existed, nurtured by a long forgetting.
The auction blocks and firebombs are gone, and yet a straight line runs from
Charleston through Tulsa to today, and though the terms have changed,
The colors too—red and blue instead of black and white—the same resentments
And divisions linger, only now without the purpose that sustained them—
As though a nation had retained its sense of grievance but had lost its cause.
Sometimes I think I brood too much on these divides, but then I listen to the radio
Or watch TV and feel the hopelessness return. It's strange how anything as abstract
As the failure of some quaint ideal of human reciprocity, of the recognition
Of ourselves in others, could reverberate so long, and yet it has. I used to
Think that history and philosophy didn't matter in the greater scheme of things:
That they were too remote from people's actual lives to make a difference,
As though the past were just another idle argument we kept repeating,
Without remembering what made it what it is. What it is

Is all around us, however difficult to see. And so the war goes on
In forms we can't quite recognize—accommodating children
Of an old obscenity still living in its lengthening shadow; or in its shade.

———

In reading and thinking about the Civil War prior to being asked to write this poem,
two things struck me, which are reflected in the poem: first, how the centennial of the war
downplayed the centrality of slavery to it; and second, how much of the lasting effects
of the war is due to its aftermath.

John Koethe

Staring Back at Us: A Gallery

Geoffrey Brock

1. Angola to Jamestown: Angela, 1619

> *Jope ... brought not any thing but 20. and odd Negroes,*
> *wch the Governor and Cape Marchant bought for victualle.*
> *—John Rolfe*

Call her the first. She wasn't alone, but hers
is the name that comes to us. Plucked from a place
somewhere along the banks of the river Kwanza,
then taken to Cape Comfort, in Virginia,

aboard two ships: first the *São João Bautista*,
a Portuguese slaver bound for Vera Cruz,
then an English privateer, the *Treasurer*
(oh bright ironical names), which traded her

for food. Such was her case.
                              Engendered there:
Fort Sumter shelled, Atlanta burned to rubble,
and Abraham Lincoln dead. (Its trading done,
her ship set sail, indifferent as a swan.)

*

[What use, to us, Leda or Zeus? We've grown
new maids, new gods—Iliums of our own.]

2. Phillis Wheatley Recalling London: 1778

On what seraphic pinions shall we move?
—Wheatley

With Granville Sharp I went to see the Tower.
We gazed upon the crowns of sires and scions
And freely spoke for one undying hour,
But fell to silence at the prisoned lions.

For crowns are signs, and signs are abstract things;
They scarcely stirred the drape on my heart's cage.
Yet when I saw those *creatures*, I felt wings
thrashing inside me, heard the call of rage.

(No other heard, of course; I was a slave
And wise to show a pretty parrot heart.
And none hear now, though I be free to rave,
Since I must make a *living* from this art.)

*

[Call her our first poet; she wasn't and was.
But look: enslaved, she was the toast of London.
Free, she couldn't publish her second book
and died a scullery maid at 31.]

3. The State of Virginia after Southampton: Christmas, 1831

> *I saw white spirits and black spirits engaged in battle,*
> *and the sun was darkened.*
> —Nat Turner

And now our nights are spent listening to noises,
a farmer writes to his sister. He recalls
the messenger's dust-trail hanging on the air
then turning to face the house his father had built,

recalls the blur of his wife in the parlor there,
his son and the cook's boy wrestling on the porch.
A corn song, a hog call, is often the germ
of nervous terror, and a cat in the dining room

will banish sleep for the night. Recalls as well
the mutter of tools and voices from the field,
and dark thin shapes that he could scarcely see,
bending and turning. Now, he dips his pen,

wanting to offer, in closing, some word of wisdom—
but sees his sister's childhood scowl, and so
merely asks again whether Cincinnati
agrees with her, and whether they've had snow.

*

[Facing a thousand tomes on the Civil War
in our local bookshop, my son asks: Why so many
books on a single subject? A long story,
I say. And if there's an end, it's just beginning.]

4. Day of Settlement: 2 Dec. 1859

I dared not refuse to obey, but at first I did not strike hard.
"Harder!" he said; "harder, harder!"
—John Brown, Jr.

We knew the rules and punishments:
three lashes for lack of diligence,
eight for disobeying mother
or telling lies... *No blood*, he'd say,

and no remission. Came a day
he started keeping my account,
as at a store. And came another
he called me to the tannery:

a Sunday, day of settlement.
I'd paid one-third the owed amount
when he, to my astonishment,
handed the blue beech switch to me,

tearful. (The greatest of my fears:
never his whippings, but those tears.)
And so it was my father paid,
himself, the balance I had owed,

our mingled blood a token of
a thing that went unnamed: his love.
This nation, too, is his bad child.
And she has failed him, made him wild

with rage and grief, and will be scourged
nearly to death before she, purged,
may rise and stand. *No blood*, I hear
him saying still, *and no remission*.

So hang him today, Virginia; cheer
his body swaying in the air—
tomorrow you will learn what's true:
hanging's a thing he's done for you.

*

[Recall who caught him, saw him hang for treason:
Robert E. Lee, he who made treason look *noble*
(and red war redder) for—well, no good reason.
File under: Looking-Glass World, Lost-Cause Rebel.]

5.   News of Fort Sumter: 13 April 1861

> *Arous'd and angry, I'd thought to beat the alarum,*
> *   and urge relentless war,*
> *But soon my fingers fail'd me …*
> *—Whitman*

He who, fresh from a Verdi opera, was humming
his way down Broadway toward the Brooklyn ferry.
He, who heard the fury of newsboys coming,
their voices, still unbroken, flailing the air,

their midnight extras flapping like gray flags.
He, who had tried to write a *poem*

                              to bind us.
Gathered with others beneath the flaring lamps
of the Metropolitan. Read that news in silence.

*

[Instead of all the statues of generals on horses
give me Walt that night at Broadway and Prince
buying a *World* or a *Times* from a shoeless orphan
and trying to make, of the kosmos disorderly,

                              sense.]

6.   William Howard Russell at Bull Run: 21 July 1861

america   as much a problem in metaphysics as
it is a nation
—Robert Hayden

They came—men in straw hats and linen coats,
wives with their parasols—in country cars
laden with city wares: with picnic baskets

and opera glasses, with pens for sketching notes.
"Bully for us!" and "Splendid!" and "My stars!"
they cried at the bright flags, the smoke, the muskets.

  (I have seen war. The horror, the sheer mess—
  Balaklava, Sebastopol. But this?)

They sipped their tea. Their brandy and Bordeaux.
Then fled like hares from what they too now know.

*

[And reenactments—Christ! Bull Run again
six months ago: hundred-degree heat,
each soldier in period wool, with a replica gun
(cheating, perhaps, with ice beneath his hat)—

and this: two sets (just one, through time's theurgy,
can see the other) of spectators! Of course!
As Freud said: first the trauma, then the urge
to rhyme it. Or Marx: first tragedy, then farce.]

7. Frank Haskell at Gettysburg: 2 July 1863

There were stern stands / And bitter runs for glory.
—Stephen Crane

The summer heat pressed down, despite the sky's
mizzling rain. We waited, where hours later
the dead would sprawl in scattered ricks, the wounded
would wait like bettors at a ticket office

for amputations. Such things I saw! Limbs
stacked like cordwood. At every house and shed
they lay—the gray-haired men, the beardless boys—
some pleading for the final panacea,

some mute, some glassily polishing tales of victory.
But first: the wait. Between our lines and theirs
lay fields of wheat, soon to be ripe. Between us,
a pasture, a peach orchard, patient corn.

Surgeons readied hospitals, stretchers. Soldiers
loitered. Several I saw curl in the dirt
to sleep. One went for water, twenty canteens
clanking like medals at his neck. Some smoked

and some told jokes and some just blinked like cows.
Then Sickles led his idiot march, and the wait
ended, and fifty thousand ramrods were thugging
their little cones, their little globes of lead ...

*

[Engendered too our weird mythologies—
history our Homer (our honer, our harshener):
Uncle Tom whipped to death for his defiance;

or Klansmen, even their horses hooded, racing
to Elsie's aid as *Ride of the Valkyries* blares;
or Scarlett picking cotton to save Tara...]

30

8. James Daniel Brock at Cold Harbor: 3 June 1864

   (What like a bullet can undeceive!)
   —Melville

   My grandfather's grandfather died at 1 AM,
   eight hours after a Union minie ball
   entered behind his left ear (the letter said)
   and ranged up. He had seen his share of slaughter,

   but nothing like what he'd have witnessed had he lived
   a few more hours: blue-black uniforms
   emerging from the cool foreshadows of dawn
   wearing the faces of men trying only to die

   as men. Pinned to each back: a name and address
   on a fresh slip of paper.
                              By the order to fire,
   they'd come so close he would have seen the breaths
   of dust, at impact, puffing from their coats.

   A few more days, and he might have stuffed his nostrils
   (many survivors did) with crushed green leaves
   as the entrenched living, awaiting further orders,
   stared at each other across ripe fields of dead.

   *

   [Six years it took me to make the time to find
   the Confederate cemetery in Fayetteville;
   it's a quarter mile from my house in the crow's mind,
   but he flies over a private, wooded hill.

   On foot, it's down, back up, around a bend
   atop a steep road marked (*oh please*) DEAD END.
   And why come now, I wondered, as I weaved
   among the headstones of the undeceived.]

9.   Monroe's Doctrine: Good Friday, 1865

The shining black mask they wear does not show a ripple
of change; they are sphinxes.
—*Mary Boykin Chesnut*

Miss Mary's diamonds was hid under Lizzie's apron.
Them Yanks was taking this and breaking that.
They mocked Miss Mary for running to us, then us
for standing by her side, though we was free.

Knowing Miss Mary's mouth, I says to her
"Don't answer back, Miss Mary—just let 'em cuss.
Don't let 'em say that you was impudent."
Them Yanks they laughed at that. But not Miss Mary.

She squinnied at me like I wasn't her Monroe.
Like them old draperies that always hung
in front of her eyes was flung aside, and she
was having trouble adjusting to the light.

Next day we gave them diamonds back like they
was garden peas, and Lizzie and me, we left.

                    *

[... and old myths taking U-turns: once beloved,
Uncle Tom, like some poor mortal in Ovid
who slights a god, becomes himself a whip;
Tara decays on the Forty Acres backlot

(only the façade was real); and the troops
(integrated now) of Colonel Kilgore
(you know: *the smell of napalm in the morning*)
blast Vietnam with *Birth of a Nation*'s score ...]

10. Grant on His Deathbed: 1885

Nations, like individuals, are punished for their transgressions.
—U.S. Grant

Have never dwelt on errors. On omissions.
Cold Harbor—order for that last assault.
The field of wounded staring back at us.
At me. Helplessly dying. Dreams' projections.

Blamed Lee for thwarting my desire to lessen—
but I, I know, I should have called a truce.
And Vicksburg too. Final attack. A fault.
(What I wanted to be was a professor.)

And that most unjust war—root of it all:
Mexico. Foretaste of command. Recall
with shame that wounded colonel. Unresisting.

My heart then like a puffed-up private boasting
he's cut the enemy's leg off.
                                        —*Not his head?*
—*Sir, someone else had cut that off already.*

*

[I used to walk up Riverside to his tomb,
and sit across the street, in Sakura Park,
in April, when the cherries were in bloom,
and read, and stare, until it got too dark.]

*The Civil War—our nation's first meaningful attempt to live up
to its own foundational ideals—is at the heart of nearly everything
that matters to me about our country. Its roots are so deep and its
ramifications so far-reaching, however, that I don't know how to speak
about it in poetry without narrowing my focus to what the Italian
poet Giovanni Pascoli called* piccole cose*—small things. With this
piece, and in part because I was writing at the behest of the National
Portrait Gallery, I fell back on a strategy I've attempted in other poems:
historical snapshots. I hope that by zooming in on a series of resonant
moments in the lives of real or imagined individuals (and even the real
ones, of course, are imagined) who were witnesses to or participants
in historical events, I might suggest something of a panorama. In
this context, the epigraphs and codas that frame each poem might be
seen as the wall text of your somewhat eccentric curator.*

Geoffrey Brock

34

I Am Silas

Yusef Komunyakaa

We worked the thorn bushes
    & front garden, hunted quail
    & jackrabbit deep into the woods,

dipped fat hens into boiling pots
    to pluck the speckled feathers,
    picked mayhaw & blackberries

beside a bog, shucked yellow corn
    into grain barrels, & horsed around
    in the snowy clover at sunset.

He was a buckaroo at sixteen
    & me seventeen when he signed up
    for the 44th Mississippi Cavalry,

& we shadowed each other
    as if of the same wet mother.
    The boy owned my surname,

but I hadn't ever said sir or mister,
    & he never called me manservant
    or slave before we teamed up

with Johnny Rebs yelling across
    the border of Cicasaw county,
    before we fought our way

to Belmont, Shiloh, Chickamauga,
    & Crooked Tree. My Bowie knife
    will never rust because the blade

knows blood. Sometimes dreams
    come out of a verse in Revelations,
    & other times out of love songs

half-whispered on a hilltop,
    or blues down from the Delta
    the whole lonely climb to West Point

winding into pine & shrub oak
    where the sapsucker & God Bird
    live by infernal grace & fire.

Once I dreamt in a canebrake
    faces of the First South Carolina,
    & I could no longer stand guard

over our sleeping shadows.
    The pale horse & the dark horse
    shook in their trace chains,

& that was when a bullet
    caught up with Andrew Chandler,
    & Yankee soldiers took us to Ohio.

To save his right leg I paid
    the camp doctor a gold piece
    sewn into his gray jacket,

& we were sent to Atlanta
in a lucky swap. Sometimes,
if you plant a red pear tree

beside an apple, the roots tangle
underneath, & it's hard to say
if you're eating apple or pear.

When we came back to runagate
crops going to seed & bedlam,
I was ready to bargain for a corner of land.

But history tried to pay me
in infamy with Judas's regalia
& a few pieces of tarnished silver.

Coda: Reflecting on a Slave in the Confederacy

When I first saw the photograph of Andrew Chandler—a young, white Confederate soldier—and Silas Chandler—a young slave—I couldn't stop thinking about the complexity of the situation—these two young southerners, slave and slave master, captured in a historical moment beyond words. Were they friends or foe, were both enslaved to time and place, had they ever laughed with almost a single voice, had one of them or both—especially Silas—ever considered the paradoxical nature of their lives?

At first, I thought I knew what Silas would say, that his anguish would be palpable and basic, but the writing of this monologue changed the speaker. Silas had to attempt to weigh (through language) the conflicted dimension of his heart, his emotions, his allegiance to the soil guiding him. I didn't wish to simplify the photograph through the slanted light of a contemporary lens. "I Am Silas" could have been longer, especially if I had collapsed the parameters of time, had projected his voice into a future outside or beyond the photograph. As one examines the history, a later photograph of Silas and his wife, Lucy, even more clearly depicts the complex reality of American social history and the politics of color. But I opted to stay close to the Silas I discovered in the agony of language, in the imagination, the Silas who fought alongside his master. And perhaps the very existence of this photograph verifies the complexity of the relationship between these two young American men. Perhaps this is only wishful thinking, yet I believe Silas possessed dominion over his psyche.

Yusef Komunyakaa

The Education of Henry Adams, Private Secretary
Mansfield Street, Portland Place, London
— Towards a Cento

Michael Schmidt

i.

Once only he saw Mr. Lincoln.
Washington, midnight, at winter's end,
A melancholy Inaugural
Ball, waltzes off-key, spurs, spittoons, and
Him a long plain figure among gowns:
Ploughed face, an air funereal in part
Due to a habit of foreboding,
In part to his too tight beige kid gloves.
No man in the Republic required
(He grimaced, saying it of himself)
More instruction than the President.

Lincoln, Seward, Sumner could not help
The greenhorn Private Secretary
With his slow *Education*; why, *they*
Knew as little as he did! (All through
The memoir his "I" is "he.") He'd read
Six long years of Law; they'd practiced it
And what they did would cost ten thousand
Million dollars and a million lives.

On April thirteen Fort Sumter fell,
The storm burst, its lightning and thunder
Rolling several hundred thousand young
Men and Henry Adams in the surf
Of a wild ocean, all helpless like

Himself but not all safe. He had time

To go observe the regiments form

Ranks by the Boston State House, gather

In the solemn April evening and

Start the march south, with the docile frowns

They'd practiced to perfection from birth.

No drums and fifes, no kind of fanfare.

He had time to go down afterwards

To the port and embrace his brother

Charles, safe-quartered for the time being

In Fort Independence, the Army

Of the Republic falling into

Line around him, boots, belts and weapons,

In resolute blue rows, their numbers

Called. Nothing was so trivial that night

As the Private Secretary in

The dark, crawling down to the Cunard

Steamboat *Niagara* to sail again

With his father the Minister for

England.

ii.

　　　　　In London Secretary

Adams carried messages, took tea,

Dictation, copied and recopied

Letters, betweentimes inching through Law

Through Blackstone, like a termite through oak.

He suffered waking nightmares. The old

Duchess Dowager of Somerset,

A harridan with castanets, forced

The Turkish Ambassador's daughter

To perform a Highland fling with him.

The gentry smirked, clapped, and stamped their feet.

That night his pride came home in ashes.

He took for granted that his business
Was obedience, discipline, silence.
He never labored so hard to learn
A language as he did to hold his
Tongue, and it affected him for life.
A habit of reticence—talking
Without meaning—cannot be broken.

In his loneliness, when the story
Of Bull Run appeared in *The Times*, he
Hugged himself tight, felt a pang so deep,
Of his own absence from the one real
Story, that he was sick for a week.
He kept the door bolted. To be dead
With—no one knew the final number.
To be dead! And, breathing, he *was* dead.
Bull Run. The cause was lost. The English
Predicted history the moment
They recognized the South. Quite soon
They'd draw the line, do the final sums.
Events happened over there, the charge,
Retreat, flags in the mud, the bodies
Heaped, the carts and mules. But *history*
Happens at a distance, happens here
Where blood dries to ink. Minutiae,
Passions, amputations, don't survive
The transit from pain to history.
The subject burns down with the houses,
The soft goods, clocks and shifts, the bird cage.
Chimneys survive, memorializing—
One, two, three, four, five—the avenue.

What might have happened if he hadn't
Taken his father's counsel and flown
The coop, a Private Secretary?

Instead like men in uniform, in

Flames, alive or dead, and not a scribe

Reading the consequences of what

Should have been his story inscribed by

Thucydides.

iii.

      Two years on, July,

In Pennsylvania. The bell's not chimed.

The rail fence holds, summer fields, the woods

Stand hospitable. The patient blue

And gray brigades find the countryside

Foreign as Palestine or Britain.

They stand to, tense, flags tight furled, breeze still.

It has not happened yet. If I don't

Put pen to paper, need it happen?

The Private Secretary dries the

Nib. On the mantle shelf the English

Clock is primed, it whirs, air waits the chime.

The voice of Longstreet rises in his

Throat, Kemper is sallow, grave Wilcox

Feels his heart dive like a fish. A jet

Of shrill sunlight bursts from Pickett's sword.

The Private Secretary wakes from

A dream of bayonets. He lies stiff.

Time to go home, father, time to go.

Which his father answers with a stare

Open and empty.

      Whitman wrote how

In some cemeteries north and south

Nearly *all* the dead are Unknown. At

Salisbury, North Carolina, the

Known are only eighty five, the un-

Known twelve thousand and twenty seven.

Eleven thousand seven hundred

Of these are buried in the furrows

The war ploughed in Lincoln's patient brow.

iv.

Many a shock was Henry Adams

To meet in the course of a long life

Spent with politicians, politics.

The profoundest lessons are not those

Of reason: they're sudden strains that warp

The mind for good. It's a dismal school

Because the lessons never finish,

The war continues as the plough turns

Up in the fields new skulls, evidence

That numbers change. No name gets added.

———————

When I came to read The Education of Henry Adams *a few years ago, I was especially taken with the chapters in which Henry's father was appointed American minister in London, made his son his private secretary, and arrived at the Court of St. James's to find that the British had just recognized the Confederacy's belligerence. The time in Britain during the Civil War was one of great anguish and privation for young Henry; for the first three years it seemed the Union cause was lost and written off with a kind of hubristic glee by the Mother Country. I imagined him as affected by his absence from a defining series of traumas in his nation's history, feeling himself defined by his absence from them. The language of the poem draws from his actual text, phrases and portions of sentences being his, hence the semi-cento form. Some of the phrases are also drawn from Faulkner, and some from Whitman. In order to avoid the elegiac tone and the iambic rhythm into which the voice tends to fall in reverie, I submitted to a severe syllabic rule, though not consistently rhyming. This was writing against the grain as much as possible. I was keen to make a poem that was American in the dignified way of Henry Adams, telling no more than the truth, but with luck no less, also. It feels a very personal poem, but who that person is is hard to say.*

Michael Schmidt

Message from the Fourth Tour

Jorie Graham

Me
ssa
ge
fro
m
Th
e
Fo
urt
h
To
ur

I will Inform
you
that I am well at
this time & that
our Co. is all
well Except two
or three Persons
our Mess all
well at Present I
hope that when
this
Reaches you it
may find you &
Friends well I
was Glad to
Hear from you
& that you was
well I Had about
given up getting

any answer from
you But Better
Late
than Never for
Indeed Miss Hal
I do love to get
News from
Home News
from Home
[*sic*] for it looks
as if that is all
the consolation
that us Soldiers
Have for we are
away from
Home & We
Have to do as
Best we can it is
& Has Bin verry
cold &
Disagreeable to
Day We cook &
Eat out Doors &
we Run to the
Table & Eat But
nearly Freeze
our Fingers
While Eating
We Have one
Stove in our
Barracks Which
Does a great

Deal of good
But one stove is
a small make
Shift for 80 or
90 men it is
verry cold
Standing guard
Especialy of
nights But If we
are Spared to get
through the war
& Return to our
Homes all will
be well I hope
that we will
leave for a
warmer climate
Soon We Have
not recd our
clothes yet But
our Major tells
us that we will
get them the
first of the next
week The 30th
Regiment Has 3
days Rations
cooked & Every
thing Ready &
will leave to
morrow for St.
Louis they

Have Recd there
guns & Success
to them I Hope
that we
will
follow
Soon I
would
Inform
you that
one of
Capt
Nobles
men Died
last night
His name
is Taylor
Four of
Nobles
men &
four of
our men
Starts
Home
with his
Remains
in the
morning
Indeed
Dear
Miss
there is

thousand
s of Poor
Soldiers
that will
see Home
& Friends
no more
in this
World
But don't
think
that I am
Home
Sick or
Dishearte
nd for
such is
not the
case for I
am only
telling
you a few
simple
Facts
+
I will
inform
you with
Pleasure
that I am
Well at
the
Present
& I hope
that
When this
Reaches
you that
it may
find you
Well I

Rec'd
your
letter of
Feb. the
8th on
the 2nd
day of
this
month &
I Have
Delayed
Answerin
g it untill
Which I
Hope you
will
Excuse
me for &
I will
Promise
to do
better in
the
future.W
e was 6
days
comeing
18 miles
through
of the
Crookede
st &
narrest
Channels
that a
Steam
Boat
Ever
went
Before
But we

Have got
through
with
about 25
Boats all
together
We Have
Some 6
or 8 gun
Boats
with us &
we are
now
Penetrati
ng into
the verry
Heart of
Dixie
Since we
Started
we Have
taken
over one
Hundred
thousand
Dollars
worth of
cotton &
taken
what
Beef &
chickens
that we
needed I
know not
where
we are
going for
certain
But what
we all

come to
war for
We Have
got to
fight
Before
we Can
come
Home I
will
Inform
you with
Pleasure
that I am
well at the
present &
I Have
Recd. no
letter
from you
Since the
about the
1st of
March I
wrote
you an
answer
on the
9th of
March &
Rec. no
Ans yet &
Since I
wrote you
last we
Have Had
consider
able
Sickness
in

our Co.
Bin
Gradualy
Sinking
Ever
Since He
is not
Exspecte
d to live I
think it
Doubtful
Whether
we stay
Here
verry
long it
Would take
about 20
Sheets of
Paper to
tell all
Have See
a great
many
large
Buildings
&
Fencing
Burned
and any
Amount
of other
Property
taken
where
Ever they
Fired on
our Boats
We
landed &
Burnt

Every
thing that
would
Burn I
Had a
light chill
yesterda
y But I
feel all
O.K. to
day We
Have
Over
4000 of
there
wounded
Here in
town I
Had
Details
out
yesterday
all Day
Burrying
there
Dead an
Officer
Come to
me this
morning
for a
nother
Detail to
Bury
more
Dead I
am
sorrow
to Inform
you that
Will

Holmes is
verry
Sick in
Hospital I
see Him
2 days
ago & not
Heard
from Him
since I
Hope
that when
this

Reaches
you that
it may
find you
well I
Have Rec.
no letter
from you
Since the
one you
Sent By
Dr Ivens
But I
Hope
that I will
Rec. a
letter
soon We
are
agoing to
have a
Pretty
long
march I
do not
Know
After we

leave
Here I
Exspect
that it
will Be
Some time Ere
we Rec.
any mail I
Have no
Idiea
How
Soon that
the mail
will
Reach us
& we will
Seldom
Have the
opportunit
y of
Sending
any letters
Back
Every
thing is
Exciteme
nt in
Camp at
Present
they are
Pulling
Down the
tents & I
Have to
Quit
writing to
Help
them I
will tell
you that I
See a

Rebel Spy
Hyng
Here on
the 8th..
He was
caught
going out
Past our
Picket
Guards &
was
arrested
&
Examined
& Papers
of Importan
ce to the
Rebels
found in
His
Possessio
n & He
was
Brought
Back &
Court
martialed
&
Sentence
d to Be
Hung
Dead By
the neck
& on the
8th.. He
was
Executed
in the
Presence
of Some
Good

Persons
His Name
was
David. O
Dodd
+
Military
Prison
Little
Rock Jan.. 8th..
10 oclock
am 1864
My Dear
Parents &
Sisters
I was
arrested
as a Spy
& Tried
&
Sentenced
to Be
Hung to
Day at 3
oclock..
the time is
fast
approachi
ng But
thank
God I am
Prepared
to Die I
Exspect
meet you
all in
Heaven I
will Soon
Be out of
this
World of

Sorrow &
Trouble I
would
like to
See you

all Before
I Die But
let God's
will Be
Done not
Ours I
Pray to
God to
give you
Strength
to Bear
your
Troubles
while in
this
World I
Hope God
will
Receive
you in
Heaven
there I
will meet
you. . .
Mother I
Know it
will Be
Hard for
you to
give up
your only
Son But
you must
Remembe
r that it is

Gods will
Good Bye
God will
give

you
Strength
to Bear
your
Troubles I
Pray that
we may
meet in
Heaven
Good Bye
God Bless
you all
Your Son
& Brother
David O.
Dodd
+

No
Roasted
Turkey
for
Dinner
Nor
Visitors
to See us
But we
Stay at
our
Camps
thinking
of Home
& of old
times &
Hopeing
for

Happier
Days to
Come
Well
Han.. I

Have my
Paper
Nearly
Filled & I
Have not
written
Half that I
could If I
Had
Room But
I cannot
tell you
all with
my Pen
for If I
did I
would
load
Down the
Mails..
Well I
must
close for
this time
Please
write
Soon &
write all
the News
&
Particular
s &
Please
Excuse
this Ill

composed
letter &

my Poor
writing & I
will try &
Do Better in
the Future If
I live &
Have my
Health I
think it the
Duty of
Every Able

Bodied man
If Necessary
to Help
Defend His
country But
I think 3
years
Sufficient
long for one
man to
Serve while
they all take
there
turns..Your
letter of

the 8th.. Inst
is Recd..
with
Pleasure
Our Co. Has
lost So
many men
In the Past

month, This
Summer
will take off
many of the
Recruits.
Dear lives I
Have no
Idea of
getting
Home

but if
Permited
to live
then I
exspect to
Return
Home &
See the
People &
Eat
Peaches
Well I
Have No
News of
Interest to
write at
this time
The
weather is
verry
warm
Here &
there is
Considera
ble
Sickness
Among
Soldiers
Citizens
&

Refugees
& many
Dieing
off. Well I
believe
that I
Have told
you all for
the
Present.
Please
write
Soon &
give all
the News
&
Particular
s & what
for & too

what
times you
are
Having &
If my
Luck is
Still
living &
on
Pleading
terms

After my
Best
wishes &
Respects
to you
Beleive
me

I decided to use, as I had done with the voices of the soldiers on Omaha, the actual voices—in this case in their own hand—of soldiers brought down from the north into the disarray of battle. There is no doubt, as these are primarily the voices of men utterly frightened by the exhaustion of their fourth tour, that I have contemporary soldiers in mind. I have focused on the wandering, sometimes enough to render one unstable, across landscape, in the north to south to north enforced reading of the poem—and how it breaks into madness (of an illuminating kind, I hope) if one tries to "break the ranks" and read sideways across the columns. Visually the columns form ranks, but in actuality they are one long snaking piece, one long march through hot and cold, ill-equipped, no idea where one is going next, diminishing idea of what for…. And then there is the desperate need to normalize the madness, to write formally about the events, and to make sure that the long thread home, letter by letter, is not broken. The flattening of the voices, the numbing, is essential to me, and painful when I think of the nonstop e-mails home today from our men in the Middle East. The need for that link, for language to work as a bridge back to sanity—peaches!—the meaning of "well"—is predominant here, so that the one inner civil war, the spy, again is bringing messages from one side to another, across the grain of the "right" trajectory the message is intended to take. To me this applies to the ultimate reasons for the war, seen now from this distance, where powerful nations around the globe have massacred their own peoples to become what they are, gigantic markets and hyperpowers. The moral grounds for this war are both obvious and obscured. I have kept the poem close to the source—the men, their written words—and tried not to rise above the mud-eye-view, except formally, to see the terrifying pattern of history.

Jorie Graham

A Soldier in the 28th Massachusetts

Eavan Boland

If his cause is American,
and his gun British—

a muzzle-loading musket
made in Enfield—

the features underneath
the blue forage cap are

Irish: a rough-cut intaglio
incised in a hidden history

of a shoreline receding
into a rainy distance

that eased out in the end
to reveal another coast

whose leaves are turning
this September evening

by the green incline
of Antietam Creek.

And if this soldier in
the 28th Massachusetts is

to hold himself in readiness
for the reckoning

with his new countrymen,
let him not remember,

not once,
his old ones. Better to forget

the deep-water harbor,
the ship waiting, his father

on the dock with a contract
ticket for his wife and son,

weeping helplessly,
in the arms of his brother.

For years I've been fascinated by the story of the 28th Massachusetts Regiment, a core part of the Irish Brigade in the Civil War. It was mainly drawn from Irish and Irish-American volunteers and saw action in many of the war's decisive battles: Fredericksburg, Gettysburg, Antietam, Chancellorsville. The soldiers had a Gaelic war cry and a green banner.

Coming from the country of origin of at least some of these soldiers, I can't help imagining the contradictions and ironies they lived with. To pull up Proust's phrase, these soldiers were like the "star-shaped crossroads in a forest." And they did indeed occupy, in his words, a place "where roads converge that have come from so many different directions."

To start with, the brigade they were part of was led by Thomas Francis Meagher, an Irish patriot born in Waterford. In his youth he had fought to bring about disunion with Britain. Transported to Australia for sedition, he escaped and fetched up in the U.S. Army. Once there, he found himself leading soldiers who were committed to preserving the union of another country.

Above all, the soldier-immigrants of the Irish Brigade signified a piercing and ironic twist of history, which became the subject of my poem. As emigrants, they would have left Ireland for America, from piers and harbors full of the noise of their grief. The partings were mortal. Family members never expected to see each other again. And yet now, as Union soldiers, they had a new and compelling cause: one that required them to take up arms against the wider family of their new country.

Eavan Boland

The Missionary Ridge Reenactment Ball

Dave Smith

Mix 'em up. I'm tired of States' rights. (1862)
Maj. General George H. Thomas, USA

All you have to do is back out of the hotel room, pass by
    battles each hall has, horses in mid-air
        flying, shell-burst, dazed glaze of corpse, go
            with the elevator's wheezing down

death's retreat, underfoot earth's green blanket
    or maybe a boy's beard, matted, eighteen
        floors over the Tennessee River's
            bayonet-flash, enough to fall

out of body when the riding ghosts greet you, two,
    soft talk like old skirmishers dreamy
        and hopeless: both are field-grade
            generals, gold-roped, butternut,

sash and saber, glass in hand, one's blue, starred
    shoulders of the Union, maze-looped,
        gauntlets worn as if for ending things,
            pistols cased. Hard to think of them

next door, raising roses, Toyotas polished, dreamers no
    blast and boil and man-scream in April
        ever called forth. I grunt hello and drop
            with these to a room of troops torqued

from still killing ground, a band's period-play sweet
        as dove-call, ladies rouged like shale that
            buckled in blood so many. Just blink—
                talkers of tactics, small gods, dance

off in breast-gleam and bows, alive in redemption,
        armies of the past, ticketed ladies, gents
            white and black, sword-point goatees.
                Oh death is this thy sting at last—

Spring plowed a body up, many bones, buttons, so
        let's have a ball, celebrate! Oh brothers,
            our fathers, absolvers, like you I want
                to pretend as glorious bodies roll by,

crinolines climbing legs, scabbards swinging, life's
        no clink of chains, no eerie bloody yells
            no bats gorging on rising bugs. But
                punch too sweet gags, the phony

swollen generals make me want to shout. What?
        I hear cicadas bomb the Southern night,
            an endless drum roll. Can't we forget,
                mouths open in disbelief, ripe smell

Spring, sun on brow bullet-shattered, crow-pecked?
        How can right play as if wrong's not
            right in any look? Let the dead stay
                in death's clothes, me in mine. If

something in me also loves this glory story, I'd be

out of here but for a moon-faced black

belle in ballgown who bangs into me,

heels snicked like a sniper's cock.

"Do I know you?" she says, aloof as the dead,

blood up, jeweled as a royal one

in Brady's photo stash, a ball queen

undreamed at Missionary Ridge

now here. Swish and grate, shovel bodies in. "You

hope so," I flirt. "Whatever's" her word,

off arm-in-arm with stars, so I wait.

The toilet's full, a dissing dowager

cheeps, "Where's your uniform, man" So I see

all that waits is sleep, but here's more,

a couple of Buds, elevator's open-up,

gowns, boots, a dream chance. It's

why, Oh Lord, this night I fall for fiddle's wail, whoop

and waltz with your rose-bridled

beauties dressed like souls come

alive, laughing, all we need, until.

I don't ask what the dead died for, but join, dance,

bowing down when music quits.

"You have a good one, man." "It's

all good, man!" Bugs, bats feeding on.

Like many who grew up among battlefields in the South, I feel the combat and suffering on that "dark and bloody ground," so present it can seem ludicrous. A decade ago I walked into the elevator of an elegant hotel in Chattanooga only to find two uniformed generals, one Confederate and one Yankee, discussing sales quotas, their day jobs, as they went to attend a ball in honor of an unidentified Civil War soldier dug up by a farmer's spring planting. The ball was the capstone event for a reenactment of the Missionary Ridge battle of 1862. Everything about it was crazy, joyful, and entirely contradictory to a point almost beyond words.

54

Dave Smith

Obscurity and Legacy

C. D. Wright

After Pura López Colomé's
Fabula disuelta, ensimismada
translated by Forrest Gander

To get up

Again

To get up

To get up on legs that stretched, strode and straddled

To unplug the mud from the end

Of the barrel

Again

Which would involve

Having hands

Or

Having *a* hand

One that understood the consistency of mud

Also

What sprang from the same consistency

The hand

That hung their door at an angle

That gawkily shore the lamb

A hand that had warmed itself in the cavities

Of a fallen man

With barely suppressed feelings of kinship

And

Revulsion

The same hand that dug a spud

From an abandoned mound

To eat with clods adhered to its skin

A hand that felt secure

Only

If not

Near peerless holding a pen

Felt

Natural, numerous, never-ending

That peeled the skin off a birch

After

The writing paper was finished

That he might inscribe

His ardency

Adieu

That would drift past as a strip of charpie

Then drift

Past a window as a clean white shirt

Bearing a husband

Freshly bathed and shaved

To get up

Again

On the undestroyed elbow

Red and raw

From the unpatched uniform

Forced into wearing

To be beside oneself

To be up on one raw red elbow

To have been forced

Into uniform

Beside blown off parts of oneself

Before

Being blown away not knowing

Parts of his lonely body were gone

His busted up bookish being fleeing

And

Once

Blown over the furrows

Once

The creek crested so little would be left

Ploughshare

Broken coulter

A few useless silver objects

From

An all but involuntary wedding

And

Now

Never

To come back

To the everlasting paradigm

Of the nearness of a known body

Leaf on leaf worm by worm snow on snow

Now

Be the woman thoroughly exhausted

Drained discolored defeated

To have gotten up

To have gone to her dresser

Before

Getting up

Again

And hoisting her hoe to the wrecked field

To have gone to her dresser

Before

Seeing her wracked visage

Now

Be the shoulders dusted as shoulders can glare

Be the credits scrolled slowly and boldly

Be the air expanding at supersonic speed

Be the windows let up and the tree

The centenarian tree dependably there

There

The tree just

Standing

There

The chestnut from which she descended

Leaf on leaf

Worm by worm

Snow on snow

Born for what resplendent reason

To irrigate this dumb mud

With his oblivious blood

Who always thought he would

Once

Again

Get up

After sucking her breast

After

Putting away his nibs

After

An unexceptional dinner with friends

Die in the snow

I was interested in a certain feature of Civil War history in the Arkansas Ozarks. That very particular part of the state, hill country where more rocks were grown than cotton, contributed the vast majority of the state's enlistees to the Union. Springing out of the Arkansas Peace Society, these men's sympathies lay with the Union, but their choice, had they one, was not to go to war. They were dubbed the "yellar rag boys." The governor gave them a choice of enlisting for the Confederacy or prison; most enlisted. I chose to imagine a soldier, forced into uniform, whose temperament, talents, and convictions made him ill-suited to rushing out to the fields to lay waste to his fellows. In my mind's eye he chose enlistment over prison, forfeiting his young life. This is backstory, not poetry.

C. D. Wright

A Civil War Suite

Paul Muldoon

1. Mathew Brady: *First Battle of Bull Run*

Wasn't it, after all, Irish riff-raff
from the docks of New Orleans,
Irish "wharf-rats,"
louts and longshoremen,

Irish toughs and roughs
(any of whom would gleefully drive a lance
through the heart
of William Tecumseh Sherman),

Irish rogues and rapscallions
culchies and munchies
who'd make up the 1st Louisiana Special Battalion
at the First Battle of Manassas
and allow Brady to become such a dab
hand at fixing that *guerre* in Daguerreotype?

2. Walt Whitman: "Cavalry Crossing a Ford"

It's hardly too much to trace the "guidon"
to the court of Eleanor of Aquitaine
and her idea of chivalry bred in the bone.
The "loitering" horses about to spill their guts
are by Keats, for sure, but Keats
out of Tennyson.
That "musical clank" is Whitman's alone.

60

3. Louis Lang: The Return of the 69th (Irish) Regiment from the Seat of War

It's been just a week since they were seen off
by Stonewall Jackson at Bull Run,
which may be why the only one to doff
his cap as if there might be an outbreak of fun
is Captain Meagher, an intimate of muddling through
since he escaped Van Diemen's Land in 1852.
You'll notice how a smoothbore gun

of the type Meagher favors for close combat
has found its way into the hands
of two brothers who are themselves in a spat
as to why a bayonet might expand
on an entry wound. Sometimes it's only by a crowded pier
we recognize what we hold dear.
The rifle points toward the linen bands

in which Sergeant Tracy's own wounds are wrapped.
His wife helps him off the baggage-cart.
Lieutenant Nugent's right arm is strapped
awkwardly in a sling. The crowd must surely part
before these six or seven drummer boys.
We can all but hear the poise
they bring to those snare drums. It's a tribute to Lang's art

that we might for a moment forget the sniper
to whom so much of this may be assigned
and focus on an *uilleann* piper
lodged in the shadows, for when it comes to what lies behind
the impulse to fade
into the background at this or any parade
the truth is he's no less blind

to us than we are to him.
I doubt somehow he'll ever make a start
on learning "The Battle Hymn
of the Republic." I suppose some might take heart
from Father O'Reilly confiding in a widow how this cup
will pass while drawing up
a slightly revised version of the heaven-chart

or the half-smile on a man who greets his child
for the first time, or the non-sniper up a tree,
or even the piper who's beguiled
Meagher into thinking Ireland might soon be free.
Stooped though he may be over his chanter and drones,
he raises everything a semitone
and allows us for the first time to see

beyond the harbor sky with its rents and rips
to what is now a no-fly dome
where we at last begin to get to grips
with the discontinued Kodachrome
of our great transports
that hardly ever put into ports
and our flag-draped coffins secretly airlifted home.

4. Emily Dickinson: *"A Slash of Blue—A Sweep of Gray"*

Here some still scout
a vineyard path
to trample out
the grapes of wrath ...
How many died
in the blood bath?
This side? That side?
You do the math.

5. Sally Mann: *Manassas*

Less the idea of what the world might be "like"
than what it is "like *photographed*"
has had us lug
over glacier-grooved

and—polished mountains what we once took
for luggage, bags of hominy grits,
barrels of pork and hardtack,
wall-to-wall crates

of wet-glass negatives,
the tackle by which we still hold on with grim
determination to our salt codfish,
the portable darkroom
in which we've yet to cure
ourselves of the idea that art is "pure" or "impure."

I was excited to be part of this project because, despite (or because of?) my Irish
background, I've always been fascinated by the Civil War, particularly as it's
been rendered by artists of various stripes. I've been particularly interested in
how writers like Whitman and Dickinson have given us a sense of the war all
the more powerful for its being "at a slant." Mathew Brady, the greatest artist
of the Civil War, comes from an Irish background, of course. I was very struck
also by the idea that the Civil War may have been better documented than the
wars, say, in Iraq and Afghanistan.

Paul Muldoon

Portrait of Abraham Lincoln
with Clouds for a Ceiling

Steve Scafidi Jr.

He could feel his pinky toe
   push through the hole
in his sock, and a rash form
      on his neck.

He saw a hawk falling from
   a locust nearby, heard
a steam train cry far off.
      He smelled the citrus

perfumes of the dignitaries
   mixing with sweat.
Mostly though he listened
      and bowed.

Not far below him under-
   ground the leg bone of a boy
from Ohio, buckles, teeth
      and rounds.

At the new cemetery
   in Pennsylvania he waited
to speak, the low clouds
      like the ceiling

of a church about to be
  torn down or replaced
with light, the crowd
        angry and somber,

the crowd pressing in,
  the appointed speaker
talking too much
        of Rome on and on

beside the bones of
  the young laid down
before him. He sensed a hair
        on his tongue, fiddled

with his ear a moment
  and then rose to speak
while the sky cleared
        and still continues

to clear—the blues
  of the sky a consecration,
a testimony for this
        new church founded

in Gettysburg, in hope
  and two hundred and seventy-
two words shouted
        over muddy earth.

Over the last several years I have been writing poems about Abraham Lincoln. Of all of the great men in our history he remains, in my opinion, the most mysterious. My aim from the beginning has been to see—through the imagination—those unrecorded, unhistorical moments in a grand life. In one poem a nude Lincoln does ten jumping jacks early in the morning beside a window. In another poem he talks to a stray dog (a Scottish terrier) who has wandered into his office. From over three hundred such poems, I am now assembling a small book of thirty-six poems. All of these poems, including the one here, are failures. In "Portrait of Abraham Lincoln with Clouds for a Ceiling" we sense a little of what Lincoln may have sensed as he waited to speak in Gettysburg. He was actually there that day; the sky did clear as the ceremony progressed. The rest is invention. He has a hair on his tongue. He smells the perfume and the sweat of Edward Everett, the main orator at this event. I took out a line that showed a vulture sitting on her egg a mile away. I never included a single pocketknife etched with the words "my son," which must be buried there by the hundreds. I never included the fever and chills of smallpox historians have discovered Lincoln was suffering. So much of that day is lost to us. This seems fitting. Lincoln's speech—his great Address—marks a furious loss of life, a loss so abundant that his eloquence aims to remind us of its enormity and its meaning. My poor poem only wants to be there with him. To be there with him on that day is probably an epic poem, not this frail thing.

Steve Scafidi Jr.

I WILL TELL YOU THE TRUTH ABOUT THIS,
I WILL TELL YOU ALL ABOUT IT

——————————

Tracy K. Smith

Carlisles Pa. Nov 21 1864

Mr abarham lincon

I wont to knw sir if you please

whether I can have my son relest

from the arme he is all the subport

I have now   his father is Dead

and his brother that wase all

the help I had   he has bean wonded

twise he has not had nothing to send me yet

now I am old and my head is blossaming

for the grave and if you dou I hope

the lord will bless you and me

tha say that you will simpethise

withe the poor   he be long to the

eight rigmat colard troops

he is a sarjent

mart welcom is his name

Benton Barracks Hospital, St. Louis, Mo. September 3, 1864

My Children

I take my pen in hand to rite you A few lines

to let you know that I have not Forgot you

be assured that I will have you if it cost me my life

on the 28th of the month 8 hundred White and

8 hundred blacke solders expects to start up

the rivore to Glasgow   when they Come

I expect to be with them and expect to get you

Both in return.

        Your Miss Kaitty said that I tried

to steal you You tell her from me that if she

meets me with ten thousand soldiers she will meet

Her enemy

        Give my love to all enquiring friends

tell them all that we are well

Camp Nelson Ky. November 26 1864

The morning was bitter cold.
It was freezing hard. I was
certain it would kill my sick child
to take him out in the cold. I told
the man in charge of the guard
that it would be the death of my boy.

I told him that my wife and children
had no place to go and that I
was a soldier of the United States.
He told me it did not make any difference.
He had orders to take all out of Camp.
He told my wife and family that if they

did not get up into the wagon he would
shoot the last one of them. My wife
carried her sick child in her arms.
The wind was blowing hard and cold
and having had to leave much of our
clothing when we left our master, my wife

with her little one was poorly clad. I followed
as far as the lines. At night I went in search.
They were in an old meeting house belonging
to the colored people. My wife and children
could not get near the fire, because
of the number of colored people huddling

by the soldiers. They had not received
a morsel of food during the whole day.
My boy was dead. He died directly
after getting down from the wagon.
Next morning I walked to Nicholasville.
I dug a grave and buried my child. I left

my family in the Meeting house—
where they still remain.

Nashville Tenn   Aug 12th 1865

Dear Wife,
I am in earnis about you comeing
and that as Soon as possiable

It is no use to Say any thing about any money
for if you come up here which I hope you will
it will be all wright as to the money matters

I want to See you and the Children very bad
I can get a house at any time I will Say the word
So you need not to fear as to that So come
wright on just as Soon as you get this

I want you to tell me the name of the baby
that was born Since I left

I am your affectionate Husband untill Death

Belair Md. Aug 25th 1864

Mr president   It is my Desire to be free   to go to see my people on the eastern shore.   my mistress wont let me   you will please let me know if we are free.   and what i can do.

Excellent Sir   My son went in the 54th regiment—

Sir, my husband, who is in Co. K. 22nd Reg't U.S. Col^d Troops
(and now in the Macon Hospital at Portsmouth with a wound in his arm)
has not received any pay since last May and then only thirteen dollars—

Sir   We The Members of Co D of the 55th Massachusetts vols
Call the attention of your Excellency to our case—

for instant look & see
that we never was freed yet
Run Right out of Slavery
In to Soldiery & we
hadent nothing atall &
our wifes & mothers most all of them
is aperishing all about & we
all are perishing our self—

i am willing to bee a soldier and serve my time
faithful like a man but i think it is hard to bee
poot off in such dogesh manner as that—

Will you see that the colored men fighting now,
are fairly treated. You ought to do this,
and do it at once, Not let the thing run along
meet it quickly and manfully. We poor oppressed ones
appeal to you, and ask fair play—

So Please if you can do any good for us do it
in the name of god—

Excuse my boldness but pleas—

your reply will settle the matter and will be appreciated,
by, a colored man who, is willing to sacrifice his son
in the cause of Freedom & Humanity—

I have nothing more to say
hoping that you will lend a listening ear
to an umble soldier
I will close—

Yours for Christs sake—

(i shall hav to send this with out a stamp
for I haint money enough to buy a stamp)

Clarksville Tenn Aug 28th 1865

Dear husband,

I guess you would like to know the reason why

that I did not come when you wrote for

and that is because I hadnot the money

and could not get it.   and if you will

send me the money. or come after me

I will come   they sent out

Soldiers from here After old Riley. and they

have got him in Jale. and one of his Sons.

and they have his brother Elias here

in Jale. dear husband If you are coming after me

I want you to come before it Get too cold.

Dear sir   I take the pleashure of writing you

A fue lins hoping that I will not ofende you

by doing so   I was raised in your state

and was sold from their when I was 31 years olde

left wife one childe Mother Brothers and sisters

My wife died about 12 years agoe and ten years

agoe I made money And went back and bought

My olde Mother and she lives with me

Seven years agoe I Maried again and commence

to by Myself and wife for two thousande dollars and

last Christmas I Made the last pay ment and I have

made Some little Money this year and I wish

to get my Kinde All with me and I will take it

as a Greate favor if you will help me to get them

fort bliss texas   March 9th 1867

My dear sister   I write you this letter to let you no
I am well   I ask of you in this letter to go and take
my boy from my wif as sh is not doing write by him
take him and keep him until I come home   if sh is
not willing to gave him up go and shoe this letter   it is
my recust for you to have him   I doe not want her
to have my child with another man   I would lik
for my child to be raised well   I will be hom next fall
if I live   a sholder stand a bad chanc but if god spars me
I will be home

78

I am 60 odd years of age—

I am 62 years of age next month—

I am about 65 years of age—

I reckon I am about 67 years old—

I am about 68 years of age—

I am on the rise of 80 years of age—

I am 89 years old—

I am 94 years of age—

I don't know my exact age—

I am the claimant in this case. I have testified before you
two different times before—

I filed my claim I think first about 12 years ago—

I am now an applicant for a pension,
because I understand
that all soldiers are entitled to a pension—

I claim pension under the general law
on account of disease of eyes
as a result of smallpox
contracted in service—

The varicose veins came on both my legs
soon after the war and the sores were there
when I first put in my claim—

I claim pension for rheumatism
and got my toe broke and I was struck
in the side with the breech of a gun
breaking my ribs—

I was a man stout and healthy
over 27 years of age when I enlisted—

When I enlisted I had a little mustache,
and some chin whiskers—

I was a green boy right off the farm and did
Just what I was told to do—

When I went to enlist the recruiting officer
said to me, your name is John Wilson.
I said, no, my name is Robert Harrison,
but he put me down as John Wilson. I was
known while in service by that name—

I cannot read nor write, and I do not know
how my name was spelled when I enlisted
nor do I know how it is spelled now
I always signed my name while in the army
by making my mark
I know my name by sound—

My mother said after my discharge that the reason
the officer put my name down as John Wilson
was he could draw my bounty—

I am the son of Solomon and Lucinda Sibley—

I am the only living child of Dennis Campbell—

My father was George Jourdan and my mother was Millie Jourdan—

My mother told me that John Barnett was my father—

My mother was Mary Eliza Jackson and my father Reuben Jackson—

My name on the roll was Frank Nunn. No sir,
it was not Frank Nearn—

My full name is Dick Lewis Barnett.
I am the applicant for pension
on account of having served
under the name Lewis Smith
which was the name I wore before
the days of slavery were over—

My correct name is Hiram Kirkland.
Some persons call me Harry and others call me Henry,
but neither is my correct name.

The text for "I WILL TELL YOU THE TRUTH ABOUT THIS, I WILL TELL YOU ALL ABOUT IT" *is composed entirely of letters and statements of African Americans enlisted in the Civil War, and those of their wives, widows, parents, and children. While the primary documents in question have been abridged, the poem preserves the original spellings and punctuation to the extent possible throughout. I relied upon the following books in composing the poem:*

Elizabeth Regosin and Donald R. Shaffer, eds., *Voices of Emancipation: Understanding Slavery, the Civil War, and Reconstruction through the U.S. Pension Bureau Files* (New York: New York University Press, 2008).

Ira Berlin and Leslie S. Rowland, eds., *Families and Freedom: A Documentary History of African-American Kinship in the Civil War Era* (New York: New Press, 1997).

Once I began reading these texts, it became clear to me that the voices in question should command all of the space within my poem. I hope that they have been arranged in such a way as to highlight certain of the main factors affecting blacks during the Civil War, chiefly: the compound effects of slavery and war upon the African American family; the injustices to which black soldiers were often subject; the difficulty black soldiers and their widows faced in attempting to claim pensions after the war; and the persistence, good faith, dignity, and commitment to the ideals of democracy that ran through the many appeals to President Lincoln, the Freedmen's Bureau, and other authorities to whom petitions were routinely addressed during and after the war. Each voice is identified and contextualized in the notes on the poem.

Tracy K. Smith

The Lost Cause ... Lost

Nikki Giovanni

The buzz of the flies
Almost were a lullaby
Rocking the dead
To a restful place

You couldn't hear the ants
Though they were
Clearly there
In the mouths
Any wound or soft
Tissue

The worms had come
Understanding those
Which were not
Trampled
Would have a great
Feast

The grasses had no
Choice but to drink
Down the blood
And bits of flesh
That was ground
Into them

In the future
It would be girls
Not field rats
Who would follow
The soldiers
Into the trenches

In the future there
Would be single
Engine airplanes
Dropping bombs

And then
In the scientific imagination
Of the 21st century
There would be men
And women
Pushing buttons
Making war clean
And Distant

But today
On This battlefield
The deadliest of This war
The Song Birds had been
Frightened off

The Turkey Buzzards retreated to watch
Deer Skunk Raccoons
Possum Groundhogs gathered
To let the smoke clear

And only the moans
Of the almost dead
And the quiet march of Lice
Gave cadence to this concert of sacrifice
For
Freedom

Some wars have to be fought. Whether a war of words or a war with bombs and guns. Whether a war of attrition or the bearing down of love upon the "sin sick soul." And clearly some wars have to be won. Should the other side prevail a great evil will befall many people. So yes this poem is an antiwar poem, but it does recognize that some things are worth fighting for. This poem also knows that war is stinky messy tragic. And that if freedom was the winner in the American Civil War then clearly those who fought against freedom were the losers. And it should be so noted.

Nikki Giovanni

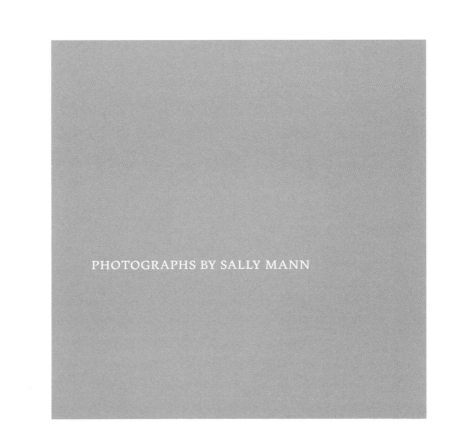

PHOTOGRAPHS BY SALLY MANN

88   *Untitled* (#1 Manassas) from *Last Measure*
Gelatin silver print with soluvar matte varnish
mixed with diatomaceous earth, 2000
Collection of the artist

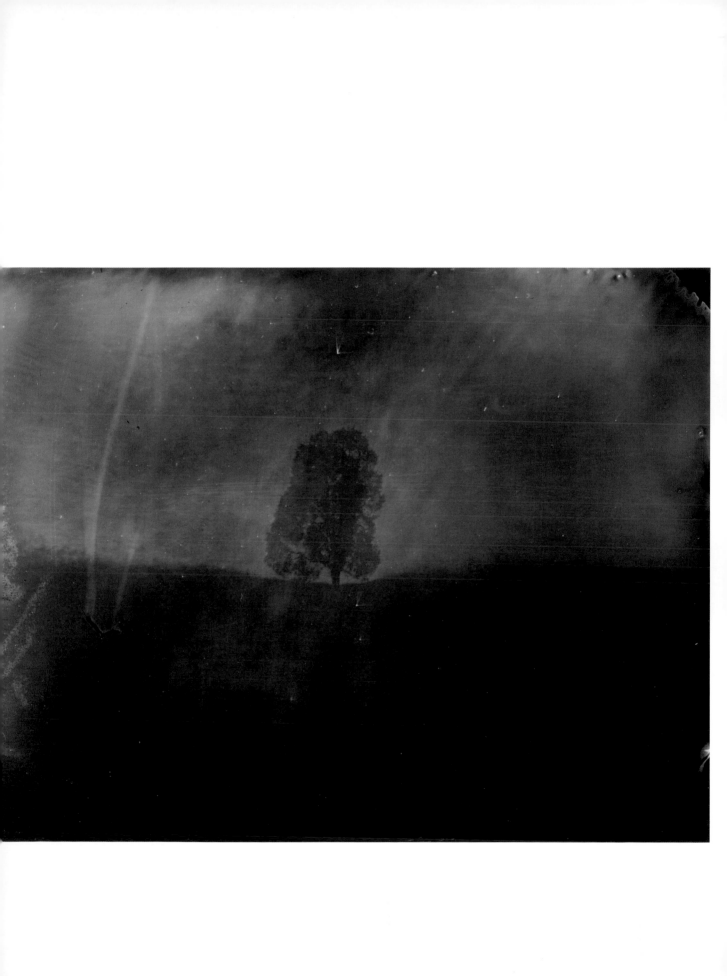

90   *Untitled* (#28 Manassas) from *Last Measure*
      Gelatin silver print with soluvar matte varnish
      mixed with diatomaceous earth, 2001
      Collection of the artist

92   *Untitled* (#5 Antietam) from *Last Measure*
      Gelatin silver print with soluvar matte varnish
      mixed with diatomaceous earth, 2000
      Collection of the artist

94   *Untitled* (#10 Fredericksburg) from *Last Measure*
Gelatin silver print with soluvar matte varnish mixed
with diatomaceous earth, 2000
Collection of the artist

96   *Untitled* (#20 Chancellorsville) from *Last Measure*
     Gelatin silver print with soluvar matte varnish
     mixed with diatomaceous earth, 2002
     Collection of the artist

98   *Untitled* (#14 Antietam) from *Last Measure*
        Gelatin silver print with soluvar matte varnish
        mixed with diatomaceous earth, 2001
        Collection of the artist

POEMS, 1854–1903

The Slave Auction

Frances Ellen Watkins Harper

The sale began—young girls were there,
  Defenseless in their wretchedness,
Whose stifled sobs of deep despair
  Revealed their anguish and distress.

And mothers stood, with streaming eyes,
  And saw their dearest children sold;
Unheeded rose their bitter cries,
  While tyrants bartered them for gold.

And woman, with her love and truth—
  For these in sable forms may dwell—
Gazed on the husband of her youth,
  With anguish none may paint or tell.

And men, whose sole crime was their hue,
  The impress of their Maker's hand,
And frail and shrinking children too,
  Were gathered in that mournful band.

Ye who have laid your loved to rest,
  And wept above their lifeless clay,
Know not the anguish of that breast,
  Whose loved are rudely torn away.

Ye may not know how desolate
  Are bosoms rudely forced to part,
And how a dull and heavy weight
  Will press the life-drops from the heart.

1854; reprinted in *Poems on Miscellaneous Subjects* (Boston and Philadelphia, 1871)

Abolition of Slavery in the District of Columbia, 1862

John Greenleaf Whittier

When first I saw our banner wave
Above the nation's council-hall,
I heard beneath its marble wall
The clanking fetters of the slave!
In the foul market-place I stood,
And saw the Christian mother sold,
And childhood with its locks of gold,
Blue-eyed and fair with Saxon blood.
I shut my eyes, I held my breath,
And, smothering down the wrath and shame
That set my Northern blood aflame,
Stood silent, where to speak was death.
Beside me gloomed the prison-cell
Where wasted one in slow decline
For uttering simple words of mine,
And loving freedom all too well.
The flag that floated from the dome
Flapped menace in the morning air;
I stood a perilled stranger where
The human broker made his home.
For crime was virtue: Gown and Sword
And Law their threefold sanction gave,
And to the quarry of the slave
Went hawking with our symbol-bird.
On the oppressor's side was power;
And yet I knew that every wrong,
However old, however strong,
But waited God's avenging hour.
I knew that truth would crush the lie,
Somehow, some time, the end would be;
Yet scarcely dared I hope to see
The triumph with my mortal eye.

But now I see it! In the sun
A free flag floats from yonder dome,
And at the nation's hearth and home
The justice long delayed is done.
Not as we hoped, in calm of prayer,
The message of deliverance comes,
But heralded by roll of drums
On waves of battle-troubled air!
Midst sounds that madden and appall,
The song that Bethlehem's shepherds knew!
The harp of David melting through
The demon-agonies of Saul!
Not as we hoped; but what are we?
Above our broken dreams and plans
God lays, with wiser hand than man's,
The corner-stones of liberty.
I cavil not with Him: the voice
That freedom's blessed gospel tells
Is sweet to me as silver bells,
Rejoicing! yea, I will rejoice!
Dear friends still toiling in the sun;
Ye dearer ones who, gone before,
Are watching from the eternal shore
The slow work by your hands begun,
Rejoice with me! The chastening rod
Blossoms with love; the furnace heat
Grows cool beneath His blessed feet
Whose form is as the Son of God!
Rejoice! Our Marah's bitter springs
Are sweetened; on our ground of grief
Rise day by day in strong relief
The prophecies of better things.
Rejoice in hope! The day and night
Are one with God, and one with them
Who see by faith the cloudy hem
Of Judgment fringed with Mercy's light!

In War Time and Other Poems (Boston, 1864)

Army Hymn ("OLD HUNDRED")

Oliver Wendell Holmes Sr.

O LORD of Hosts! Almighty King!
Behold the sacrifice we bring
To every arm thy strength impart,
Thy spirit shed through every heart!

Wake in our breasts the living fires,
The holy faith that warmed our sires;
Thy hand hath made our Nation free;
To die for her is serving Thee.

Be Thou a pillared flame to show
The midnight snare, the silent foe;
And when the battle thunders loud,
Still guide us in its moving cloud.

God of all Nations! Sovereign Lord
In thy dread name we draw the sword,
We lift the starry flag on high
That fills with light our stormy sky.

From treason's rent, from murder's stain,
Guard Thou its folds till Peace shall reign,—
Till fort and field, till shore and sea,
Join our loud anthem, PRAISE TO THEE!

The Atlantic Monthly, June 1861

Cavalry Crossing a Ford

Walt Whitman

A LINE in long array, where they wind betwixt green islands,
They take a serpentine course, their arms flash in the sun—
    hark to the musical clank,
Behold the silvery river, in it the splashing horses, loitering
    stop to drink,
Behold the brown-faced men, each group, each person a
    picture, the negligent rest on the saddles,
Some emerge on the opposite bank, others are just entering
    the ford—while,
Scarlet, and blue, and snowy white,
The guidon flags flutter gayly in the wind.

Drum-Taps (New York, 1865)

Shiloh: A Requiem (April, 1862)

Herman Melville

Skimming lightly, wheeling still,
    The swallows fly low
Over the field in clouded days,
    The forest-field of Shiloh—
Over the field where April rain
Solaced the parched ones stretched in pain
Through the pause of night
That followed the Sunday fight
    Around the church of Shiloh—
The church so lone, the log-built one,
That echoed to many a parting groan
    And natural prayer
    Of dying foemen mingled there—
Foemen at morn, but friends at eve—
    Fame or country least their care
(What like a bullet can undeceive!)
    But now they lie low,
While over them the swallows skim,
    And all is hushed at Shiloh.

Battle-Pieces and Aspects of the War (New York, 1866)

Ode: Graves of the Confederate Dead

Henry Timrod

I
Sleep sweetly in your humble graves,
Sleep, martyrs of a fallen cause;
Though yet no marble column craves
The pilgrim here to pause.

II
In seeds of laurel in the earth
The blossom of your fame is blown,
And somewhere, waiting for its birth,
The shaft is in the stone!

III
Meanwhile, behalf the tardy years
Which keep in trust your storied tombs,
Behold! your sisters bring their tears,
And these memorial blooms.

IV
Small tributes! but your shades will smile
More proudly on these wreaths to-day,
Than when some cannon-moulded pile
Shall overlook this bay.

V
Stoop, angels, hither from the skies!
There is no holier spot of ground
Than where defeated valor lies,
By mourning beauty crowned!

Charleston (S.C.) Daily Courier, July 18, 1866; revised July 23, 1866

My Triumph lasted till the Drums . . .

Emily Dickinson

108

My Triumph lasted till the Drums
Had left the Dead alone
And then I dropped my Victory
And chastened stole along
To where the finished Faces
Conclusion turned on me
And then I hated Glory
And wished myself were They.

What is to be is best descried
When it has also been—
Could Prospect taste of Retrospect
The tyrannies of Men
Were Tenderer—diviner
The transitive toward.
A Bayonet's contrition
Is nothing to the Dead.

Poem number 1227, in Thomas H. Johnson, ed., *The Complete Poems of Emily Dickinson* (Cambridge, Mass., The Belknap Press of Harvard University Press, 1955).

Our Orders

Julia Ward Howe

WEAVE no more silks, ye Lyons looms,
  To deck our girls for gay delights!
The crimson flower of battle blooms,
  And solemn marches fill the night.

Weave but the flag whose bars to-day
  Drooped heavy o'er our early dead,
And homely garments, coarse and gray,
  For orphans that must earn their bread!

Keep back your tunes, ye viols sweet,
  That poured delight from other lands!
Rouse there the dancer's restless feet:
  The trumpet leads our warrior bands.

And ye that wage the war of words
  With mystic fame and subtle power,
Go, chatter to the idle birds,
  Or teach the lesson of the hour!

Ye Sibyl Arts, in one stern knot
  Be all your offices combined!
Stand close, while Courage draws the lot,
  The destiny of human kind.

And if that destiny could fail,
  The sun should darken in the sky,
The eternal bloom of Nature pale,
  And God, and Truth, and Freedom die!

The Atlantic Monthly, July 1861

Dirge for a Soldier

George H. Boker

CLOSE his eyes; his work is done!
What to him is friend or foeman,
Rise of moon, or set of sun,
Hand of man, or kiss of woman?
Lay him low, lay him low,
In the clover or the snow!
What cares he? he can not know:
Lay him low!

As man may, he fought his fight,
Proved his truth by his endeavor;
Let him sleep in solemn night,
Sleep forever and forever.
Lay him low, lay him low,
In the clover or the snow!
What cares he? he can not know:
Lay him low!

Fold him in his country's stars,
Roll the drum and fire the volley!
What to him are all our wars,
What but death bemocking folly?
Lay him low, lay him low,
In the clover or the snow!
What cares he? he can not know:
Lay him low!

Leave him to God's watching eye,
Trust him to the hand that made him.
Mortal love weeps idly by:
God alone has power to aid him.
Lay him low, lay him low,
In the clover or the snow!
What cares he? he can not know:
Lay him low.

Poems of the War (Boston, 1864)

All Quiet Along the Potomac Tonight (The Picket Guard)

Ethel Lynn Beers

"All quiet along the Potomac to-night!"
    Except here and there a stray picket
Is shot, as he walks on his beat, to and fro,
    By a rifleman hid in the thicket.
'Tis nothing! a private or two now and then
    Will not count in the news of a battle;
Not an officer lost, only one of the men
    Moaning out, all alone, the death rattle.
All quiet along the Potomac to-night!
    Where the soldiers lie peacefully dreaming;
And their tents in the rays of the clear autumn moon,
    And the light of their camp-fires are gleaming.
A tremulous sigh, as a gentle night-wind
    Through the forest leaves slowly is creeping;
While the stars up above, with their glittering eyes,
    Keep guard o'er the army sleeping.
There's only the sound of the lone sentry's tread
    As he tramps from the rock to the fountain,
And thinks of the two on the low trundle bed,
    Far away, in the cot on the mountain.
His musket falls slack, his face, dark and grim,
    Grows gentle with memories tender,
As he mutters a prayer for the children asleep,
    And their mother—"may heaven defend her!"
The moon seems to shine forth as brightly as then—
    That night, when the love, yet unspoken,
Leaped up to his lips, and when low-murmured vows
    Were pledged to be ever unbroken.
Then drawing his sleeve roughly over his eyes,
    He dashes off tears that are welling;
And gathers the gun closer up to his breast
    As if to keep down his heart's swelling.

He passes the fountain, the blasted pine-tree,
　　And his footstep is lagging and weary;
Yet onward he goes, through the broad belt of light,
　　Towards the shades of the forest so dreary.
Hark! was it the night-wind that rustled the leaves?
Was it the moonlight so wondrously flashing?
It looked like a rifle: "Ha! Mary, good-by!"
And his life-blood is ebbing and plashing.
"All quiet along the Potomac to-night!"
No sound save the rush of the river;
While soft falls the dew on the face of the dead,
And the picket's off duty forever.

Harper's Weekly, November 1861

The Virginians of the Valley

Francis Orray Ticknor

The knightliest knights of the knightly race
Who, since the days of old,
Have kept the lamp of chivalry
Alight in hearts of gold:
The kindliest of the kindly band
Who, rarely hating ease,
Yet rode with Spottswood round the land,
And Raleigh round the seas;

Who climbed the blue Virginia hills
Against embattled foes,
And planted there, in valleys fair,
The lily and the rose;
Whose fragrance lives in many lands,
Whose beauty stars the earth,
And lights the hearths of happy homes
With loveliness and worth.

We thought they slept! the sons who kept
The names of noble sires,
And slumbered while the darkness crept
Around their vigil-fires;
But aye the "Golden Horseshoe" Knights
Their old Dominion keep,
Whose foes have found enchanted ground,
But not a knight asleep!

Michelle Cutliff Ticknor, ed., *The Poems of Francis Orray Ticknor*
(New York and Washington, 1911), 1861

A Year's Casualties

Ambrose Bierce

Slain as they lay by the secret, slow,
Pitiless hand of an unseen foe,
Two score thousand old soldiers have crossed
The river to join the loved and lost.
In the space of a year their spirits fled,
Silent and white, to the camp of the dead.

One after one, they fall asleep
And the pension agents awake to weep,
And orphaned statesmen are loud in their wail
As the souls flit by on the evening gale.
O Father of Battles, pray give us release
From the horrors of peace, the horrors of peace!

Shapes of Clay (San Francisco, 1903)

PHOTOGRAPHS BY ALEXANDER GARDNER

118   *Breaking Camp, Brandy Station, Virginia*
Albumen print, 1864
Photographic History Collection,
National Museum of American History,
Smithsonian Institution

120   *Quarters of Men in Fort Sedgwick, generally known as Fort Hell*
Albumen print, 1865
Photographic History Collection,
National Museum of American History,
Smithsonian Institution

122   *Ruins of Arsenal, Richmond, Virginia*
Albumen print, 1865
Photographic History Collection,
National Museum of American History,
Smithsonian Institution

124   *A Burial Party, Cold Harbor, Virginia*
Albumen print, 1865
Photographic History Collection,
National Museum of American History,
Smithsonian Institution

126   *Appomattox Station, Virginia*
Albumen print, 1865
Photographic History Collection,
National Museum of American History,
Smithsonian Institution

128   *Incidents of the War: Guides to the Army of the Potomac*
Albumen print, 1862
Smithsonian American Art Museum
Museum purchase through the
Julia D. Strong Endowment

Biographies

MODERN POETS

EAVAN BOLAND was born in Ireland and now teaches at Stanford University. She has published many books of poetry, including *Outside History: Selected Poems (1990), In Time of Violence* (1994), and *Domestic Violence* (2007). She has also written critical studies of poetry and the poetic tradition, including *Object Lessons: The Life of the Woman and the Poet in Our Time* (1995) and, most recently, *A Journey With Two Maps* (2011).

GEOFFREY BROCK's first book of poetry, *Weighing Light*, appeared in 2005, and his second, *Voices Bright Flags*, is forthcoming. He is the editor of *The FSG Book of Twentieth-Century Italian Poetry* and the translator of several books from Italian, including Cesare Pavese's *Disaffections: Complete Poems, 1930–1950*. His awards include fellowships from the National Endowment for the Arts, the Guggenheim Foundation, and the Cullman Center for Scholars and Writers at the New York Public Library. He teaches creative writing and translation at the University of Arkansas.

NIKKI GIOVANNI was born in Knoxville, Tennessee, and grew up in Lincoln Heights, an all-black suburb of Cincinnati, Ohio. She and her sister spent their summers with their grandparents in Knoxville, and she graduated with honors from Fisk University, her grandfather's alma mater, in 1968. She published her first book of poetry, *Black Feeling, Black Talk*, that same year. Within the next year she published a second book, thus launching her career as a writer. The author of some thirty books for both adults and children, Giovanni is a University Distinguished Professor at Virginia Tech in Blacksburg, Virginia.

JORIE GRAHAM is the author of twelve collections of poetry, including *The Dream of the Unified Field,* which won the Pulitzer Prize, and most recently *Place* (HarperCollins / Carcanet). Other recent books include *Overlord*, a collection of poems that meditate on the events surrounding D-Day on Omaha Beach, as she spent ten years living on those grounds in Normandy. She teaches at Harvard University.

LINES IN LONG ARRAY / BIOGRAPHIES

JOHN KOETHE is the author of nine books of poetry, including *Domes* (1973), which received the Frank O'Hara Award; *Falling Water* (1997), which received the Kingsley Tufts Poetry Award; and *Ninety-Fifth Street* (2009), which received the Lenore Marshall Prize. His most recent book is *ROTC Kills* (2012), and he is also the author of books on Wittgenstein and skepticism. He is Distinguished Professor of Philosophy Emeritus at the University of Wisconsin-Milwuakee.

YUSEF KOMUNYAKAA's thirteen books of poetry include *Taboo, Dien Cai Dau, Neon Vernacular*—for which he received the Pulitzer Prize—*Warhorses,* and most recently *The Chameleon Couch.* His many honors include the William Faulkner Prize (Université de Rennes, France), the Ruth Lilly Poetry Prize, the Kingsley Tufts Poetry Award, and the 2011 Wallace Stevens Award. His plays, performance art, and libretti have been performed internationally and include *Saturnalia, Testimony,* and *Gilgamesh.* He teaches at New York University.

PAUL MULDOON is the author of eleven collections of poetry, including *Moy Sand and Gravel,* for which he won a Pulitzer Prize. A fellow of the Royal Society of Literature and the American Academy of Arts and Letters, he is also an honorary fellow of Hertford College, Oxford. He is the Howard G. B. Clark University Professor at Princeton and poetry editor of the *New Yorker.*

STEVE SCAFIDI JR. is the author of *Sparks from a Nine-Pound Hammer* (2001), *For Love of Common Words* (2006), and *The Cabinetmaker's Window* (2014) with Louisiana State University Press, and a fourth collection of poems concerning the life of Abraham Lincoln, which will appear with the University of Arkansas Press in the spring of 2014. He works as a cabinetmaker and lives with his family in Summit Point, West Virginia.

Born in Mexico, MICHAEL SCHMIDT studied at Harvard and at Wadham College, Oxford. He is professor of poetry at Glasgow University and writer-in-residence at St. John's College, Cambridge. He is a founder (1969) and editorial and managing director of Carcanet Press Limited and a founder (1972) and general editor of *PN Review.* An anthologist, translator, critic, and literary historian, he is a fellow of the Royal Society of Literature and received an O.B.E. in 2006 for services to poetry. Recent publications include *Collected Poems* (2009) and a forthcoming history of the novel in English for Harvard University Press, a companion volume to his *Lives of the Poets* (Knopf, 1999) and *The First Poets* (Knopf, 2006).

DAVE SMITH's most recent book of poems is *Hawks on Wires* (Louisiana State University Press, 2011). He has published more than a dozen volumes of poetry, including *Little Boats, Unsalvaged: Poems 1992–2004,* and *The Wick of Memory: New and Selected Poems, 1970–2000,* which was chosen as the *Dictionary of Literary Biography*'s Book of the Year in Poetry. He is the Elliott Coleman Professor of Poetry at Johns Hopkins University.

TRACY K. SMITH is the author of three books of poetry: *Life on Mars*, which was awarded the 2012 Pulitzer Prize; *Duende*, recipient of the 2006 James Laughlin Award from the Academy of American Poets; and *The Body's Question*, selected for the 2002 Cave Canem Poetry Prize. Smith teaches creative writing at Princeton University and is currently at work on a memoir.

C. D. WRIGHT is the author of more than a dozen books, most recently, *One with Others,* a finalist for the National Book Award and winner of the National Book Critics Circle Award and the Lenore Marshall Prize. Her book *Rising, Falling, Hovering* won the 2009 International Griffin Poetry Prize. With photographer Deborah Luster she published *One Big Self: Prisoners of Louisiana,* which won the Lange-Taylor Prize from the Center for Documentary Studies at Duke University. On a fellowship for writers from the Wallace Foundation, Wright curated a "Walk-in Book of Arkansas," a multimedia exhibition that toured throughout her native state. In 2004 she was named a MacArthur Fellow, and in 2005 she received the Robert Creeley Award. Wright is on the faculty at Brown University. She is married to poet Forrest Gander and they have a son, Brecht.

EARLY POETS

ETHEL LYNN BEERS (1827–1879), from Goshen, New York, was a poet and a writer of sentimental Victorian stories, best known for the poem included here, "All Quiet Along the Potomac Tonight" ("The Picket Guard"). She died the day after the publication of her only book of collected poems.

AMBROSE BIERCE (1842–d. after 1913), a social critic, writer, and poet known for his mordant take on human nature and society, served in the Civil War and was seriously wounded at the Battle of Kennesaw Mountain (1864). His best-known Civil War writing was "An Occurrence at Owl Creek Bridge."

GEORGE H. BOKER (1823–1890), poet and playwright, was born into a wealthy Philadelphia banking family and began his literary career at Princeton. He published his first book of poems in 1848. A staunch Republican, he also served as minister to Turkey and Russia during Ulysses S. Grant's administration.

Now one of America's most famous and innovative poets, EMILY DICKINSON (1830–1886) was virtually unknown during her lifetime, publishing only a few poems. While her work appears as hermetic as her isolated existence in Amherst, Massachusetts, she was preternaturally attuned to American culture and the great events of her day, incorporating events like the Civil War into her allusive and distinctive verse.

FRANCES ELLEN WATKINS HARPER (1825–1911), abolitionist, writer, and poet, was one of the most important African American writers in the nineteenth century, publishing her first book of poems at age twenty and her first novel when she was sixty-seven. She was also prominent as a teacher and activist in the abolitionist, women's rights, and temperance movements.

Doctor, professor, and writer OLIVER WENDELL HOLMES SR. (1809–1894), was one of the more important figures in the American Renaissance and served as the hub of a literary society centered in Cambridge, Massachusetts. The Civil War served as an inspiration for much of his best writing.

JULIA WARD HOWE (1819–1910), abolitionist and social reformer, is best known for penning "The Battle Hymn of the Republic" as well as other patriotic songs such as "John Brown's Body." After the war she became a leader in the women's rights movement.

During his lifetime HERMAN MELVILLE (1819–1891) was best known for his exotic and titillating travel novels about adventures in the South Seas. When he turned to darker fiction, including *Moby-Dick* (1851), he lost an audience that he never regained. Only in the mid-twentieth century was his importance in American letters recognized. Melville also wrote poetry, although his attempts to become a great American poet through his verse epic *Clarel* (1876) was a popular and critical failure.

FRANCIS ORRAY TICKNOR (1822–1874), a Georgia physician and writer, is best known for his poem "Little Giffen," about a wounded Confederate soldier. Several volumes of Ticknor's poetry were published posthumously.

HENRY TIMROD (1828–1867), a South Carolina lawyer, teacher, and literary figure, started publishing poems as an undergraduate. He became best known for his war poems, which combined Victorian sentimentality with a fervor for the southern cause of independence from the North. Curiously, his lyrics influenced the songwriting of Bob Dylan to the point where Dylan was accused of "borrowing" from the southerner.

WALT WHITMAN (1819–1892) was America's first great poet but never attained that status during his lifetime. His *Leaves of Grass* (1855 and subsequent editions) sold poorly, and his ecstatic verse was received with bewilderment by the public, in part because he was too "earthy" for Victorian America. During the Civil War, he lived in Washington, nursed wounded soldiers, and observed the war in both prose and poetry; *Drum Taps* collects his war poems.

JOHN GREENLEAF WHITTIER (1807–1892) was a Quaker, an ardent abolitionist and social reformer, and a poet well known for his verse about his native New England as well as for the causes he supported. He was one of the founders of *The Atlantic Monthly* and a prolific contributor to the magazine.

PHOTOGRAPHERS

ALEXANDER GARDNER (1821–1882) was one of the premier photographers of the American Civil War. Born in Paisley, Scotland, he immigrated to New York, where he found work with photographer Mathew Brady. In 1858 he took charge of Brady's studio in Washington, D.C., and he opened his own studio in that city in 1863. Gardner and his assistants completed the most comprehensive photographic record of the Civil War. One result of this work was the publication in 1866 of his two-volume *Gardner's Photographic Sketch Book of the War*. After the war Gardner made two trips west of the Mississippi River before retiring his photographic practice to found an insurance company in Washington.

SALLY MANN is a photographer who lives in Lexington, Virginia. Her work has been the subject of numerous critically praised exhibitions and books, including *Immediate Family* (1992), *Still Time* (1994), *Deep South* (2005), and *Proud Flesh* (2009). Her landscapes of Civil War battle sites were first featured in the book *What Remains* (2003). A former Guggenheim fellow and a recipient of three National Endowment for the Arts fellowships, she is represented in many leading private and museum collections.

EDITORS

FRANK H. GOODYEAR III is the co-director of the Bowdoin College Museum of Art in Brunswick, Maine. He was previously curator of photographs at the Smithsonian's National Portrait Gallery. He is the author of four books: *Red Cloud: Photographs of a Lakota Chief* (2003); *Zaida Ben-Yusuf: New York Portrait Photographer* (2008); *Faces of the Frontier: Photographic Portraits from the American West, 1845–1924* (2009); and *A President in Yellowstone: The F. Jay Haynes Photographic Album of Chester Arthur's 1883 Expedition* (2013).

DAVID C. WARD is a historian at the National Portrait Gallery. His publications include *Charles Willson Peale: Art and Selfhood in the Early Republic* (University of California, 2004); *Hide/Seek: Difference and Desire in American Portraiture* (Smithsonian Books, 2010); and a book of poems, *Internal Difference* (Carcanet Press, 2011).

Acknowledgments

This book, and the creation of these poems, would not have been possible without generous grants from the Smithsonian Institution's Consortium for Understanding the American Experience, headed by Michelle Delaney. This book is published in conjunction with the Smithsonian's commemoration of the 150th anniversary of the Civil War.

At the National Portrait Gallery we would like to thank Amy Baskette, who handled bureaucratic tasks with patience and aplomb, and Dru Dowdy, who edited and organized the manuscript, as well as managed the publication process. The book was designed by Antonio Alcalá at Studio A in Alexandria. Eleanor Harvey, chief curator at the Smithsonian American Art Museum, took time out from her own Civil War project to talk with us, as did other colleagues at the Smithsonian, including Shannon Perich, Jennifer Jones, and Harry Rubenstein.

Index of Poets and Artists